Speak Love Revolution

Gabby –
Happy 2014!
Our time together has
only just begun. 😊 May
your new year be filled with
blessings, laughter, & love. Thank
you for letting me be part
of it. – Wendy

Other books from Annie F. Downs

Perfectly Unique: Praising God from Head to Foot

Speak Love: Making Your Words Matter

Speak Love Revolution

---

30 Devotions that Will Change Your World

---

annie f. downs

ZONDERVAN®

ZONDERVAN

Speak Love Revolution
Copyright © 2013 by Annie F. Downs

This title is also available as a Zondervan ebook.
Visit www.zondervan.com/ebooks.

Requests for information should be addressed to:
Zonderkidz, 5300 Patterson Ave SE, Grand Rapids, Michigan 49530

ISBN 978-0-310-74378-1

Published in association with KLO Publishing Service, LLC (www.KLOPublishing.com).

Cover design: Cindy Davis
Interior design: Ben Fetterley and Sarah Molegraaf

Printed in the United States of America

13 14 15 16 17 18 19 20 21 /DCI/ 21 20 19 18 17 16 15 14 13 12 11 10 9 8 7 6 5 4 3 2 1

Contents

Dear friend,

I have an interesting invitation for you.

Want to join me in a revolution? No, we won't use guns or sing *Les Misérables* songs over a barricade, but we are going to fight.

In the past few months, I have grown to appreciate the power God has given each of us with our words. Proverbs says that words have the power of life and death, and as I look back over my life, I'm seeing how true that has always been. (I know, I know. The fact that a Bible verse is true is nothing to stop the presses over since the *whole* Bible is true, but I wanted to state it anyway.)

So I want you to join me in a word revolution. I want us to be the generation of women who focus on bringing life, not death, with our words. Call me crazy, but what if we were the generation of women who ended the mean girl mentality? What if we changed the world like that? Can you imagine it?

I can. I can see a world where people pause before they speak because what used to be okay to say is no longer okay. And I can see girls filling each other with encouragement. I can see it. And, y'all, I want to be a part of that.

I want you to be a part of it too.

So here's how this word revolution works. I've given you thirty days of short devotionals that you can read just before you head out the door or right before you fall asleep. For each day, I've included

- The topic for that day
- A verse from the Bible
- A few thoughts from me
- A prayer you can say to God as you digest that day's devotion, expound on it in your journal, or whatever you want—it's just a guiding tool

- A revolt—an action you can take that very day to be part of the word revolution

Several days encourage you to use your words to make a difference through social media outlets. If you don't have any or all of those social media outlets, no biggie! Just do in real life what the day's revolt says to do on the computer (encourage someone, say a Scripture verse out loud, etc.).

Also, I must tell you—I don't dive fifty feet deep down into each topic. I just give some thoughts, some challenges, and some encouragement.[1] Pop over to my Facebook page (Facebook.com/annieblogs) and let's have a discussion there!

Thanks for joining me in this revolution. I can't wait to hear how it goes for you. I'm praying for you today—that you would stand up for truth, that you would use your words to give life, and that you would see how God can use you and your words to change lives. And maybe the world.

Let's revolt, y'all!

Sincerely,

Annie

(P.S.: We're gonna memorize one short Scripture together. Hopefully, one of many for you. Keep reading … it's next.)

---

1. *If you do want to go deeper on any of the things we discuss in these thirty days, talk to your parents, youth leaders, small group leaders, or any Christian adult you trust.*

Memory
Verse

Proverbs 12:18

Reckless words pierce like a sword,
but the tongue of the wise brings healing.

Your Words Matter

Proverbs 18:21

The tongue has the power of life and death.

The Bible can be so serious. Life and death, really? But it is true. I see that truth in my life ... Do you see it in yours? I can tell you story after story of how someone's words gave me life and how someone's words killed something in me.

As Christian gals trying to figure out this walk with God, we need to see how revolutionary our words can be. In Genesis 1:3, God SPOKE, and there was light. We are made in His image, so we have the power to create with our words too.

For years women have struggled to use their words to give life and deny the temptation to tear others down with what they say. My prayer for you is that after thirty days, you will revolt against that temptation and change the world ... one life-giving word at a time.

Your words matter, my friend. I can't wait to see you live it out.

Talk to God

Dear God, I'm stepping into this journey with an open mind and an open heart. I want to use my words for good. I really do. I recognize the power I have, so would You teach me how to use it? Make me more like You in these next thirty days. May the words of my mouth and the meditation of my heart be pleasing to You (Psalm 19:14).

Revolt

For today, just listen to yourself. Don't judge yourself or edit what you say. Just listen. Hear how you use your words. Listen to the conversations where you are inclined to get snippy or mad. Listen to the people whom you find it easy to love with your words, and notice the ones who make it difficult.

Wanna tell your friends that you're embarking on a word revolution? Use the hashtag #SpeakLove on Instagram, Facebook, Twitter, and Pinterest.

Poor Eve

Genesis 3:1–7 Temptation

Now the serpent was more crafty than any of the wild animals the Lord God had made. He said to the woman, "Did God really say, 'You must not eat from any tree in the garden'?"

The woman said to the serpent, "We may eat fruit from the trees in the garden, but God did say, 'You must not eat fruit from the tree that is in the middle of the garden, and you must not touch it, or you will die.'"

"You will not surely die," the serpent said to the woman. "For God knows that when you eat of it your eyes will be opened, and you will be like God, knowing good and evil."

When the woman saw that the fruit of the tree was good for food and pleasing to the eye, and also desirable for gaining wisdom, she took some and ate it. She also gave some to her husband, who was with her, and he ate it. Then the eyes of both of them were opened, and they realized they were naked; so they sewed fig leaves together and made coverings for themselves.

Poor Eve. She was the first woman deceived by words—but not the last. God had said one thing, Satan said another … and

Eve fell for Satan's lies. The power of words changed everything for us. EVERYTHING. Sin entered the world, shame entered our world, and Jesus paid for it with His life.

Why start this devotional on such a bummer note? Because I want you to know that your struggle to know truth from lies and with words in general, is something you come by honestly.

It's hard to speak truth and love if your mind is full of lies. And Satan is the one who is always trying to kill, steal, and destroy (John 10:10). It's time to stop listening to the lies so you can speak the truth.

I struggled with this so much as a teenager—my mind was full of lies ("You are so ugly," "No one really loves you," etc.), so I know what that's like.

But we have to choose truth. If Eve would have chosen the true words from God, imagine how different our lives would be.

Talk to God

God, please show me any lies I believe about myself that are keeping me from speaking truth. Reveal those to me. I want to speak truth and love into the world. Help me to hear and believe Your voice over the voices that try to deceive me.

Revolt

Choose to believe God's truth today. Write the following verse on a note card and hang it on your bathroom mirror:

"But you are a chosen people, a royal priesthood, a holy nation, a people belonging to God, that you may declare the praises of him who called you out of darkness into his wonderful light." (1 Peter 2:9)

Queen Esther

Esther 7:3–4

Then Queen Esther answered, "If I have found favor with you, O king, and if it pleases your majesty, grant me my life—this is my petition. And spare my people—this is my request. For I and my people have been sold for destruction and slaughter and annihilation. If we had merely been sold as male and female slaves, I would have kept quiet, because no such distress would justify disturbing the king."

It would take a ton of time to tell you the whole Esther story (but it is a good one, y'all, so you should read the whole book of Esther sometime). For our purposes, I just want to talk about her words. Here's the thing—the Bible is *full* of people who use their words well and those who don't. Queen Esther did it right—her words saved thousands of Jewish people.

She was brave with her words. Very brave. The very conversation she had with the king could have cost her life. Instead, God used her words to rescue other lives. Part of speaking life is knowing when to be brave with your words.

Want to be part of a word revolution? Be brave. Talk about

Jesus to people who don't know Him. Say something nice to the girl who is always mean. Stand up for someone who's being bullied and stand by their side. Stop lies when you hear them with something as simple as, "That's not true." Ask your youth minister if y'all can go on a mission trip to a place that is outside your comfort zone. Tell your parents if a friend is cutting herself.

I promise you this—one teenage girl saying a brave thing can absolutely change the world. It could be you.

Talk to God

God, fill me with wisdom so I will know when to be brave with my words. Give me that extra ounce of courage when I need to say the brave thing. I want to do it. I want to be brave with my words. Just help me know when and how.

Revolt

Say something brave today. You can do it. I know you can. Even if it is just saying "I love you" to your family or "I am a Christian" or "Thanks for letting me sit with you at lunch." You know the brave thing you need to do. Practice today.

Power in the Desert

Matthew 4:1–7

Then Jesus was led by the Spirit into the desert to be tempted by the devil. After fasting forty days and forty nights, he was hungry. The tempter came to him and said, "If you are the Son of God, tell these stones to become bread."

Jesus answered, "It is written: 'Man does not live on bread alone, but on every word that comes from the mouth of God.'"

Then the devil took him to the holy city and had him stand on the highest point of the temple. "If you are the Son of God," he said, "throw yourself down. For it is written:

'He will command his angels concerning you, and they will lift you up in their hands, so that you will not strike your foot against a stone.'"

Jesus answered him, "It is also written: 'Do not put the Lord your God to the test.'"

There is so much to this story—so many topics we could talk about especially, because, you know, it's *Jesus.* But when we are thinking about using our words to create life, this story is another example of truth versus lies and how words can be life.

Jesus was faced (*like face to face*) with temptation from Satan. But Jesus stood up against the lies and spoke truth into the situation. Every time Satan offered something to Jesus, Jesus responded with a Scripture. Jesus didn't have a copy of the Bible right in front of Him—He *knew* the verses.

How cool is that? God wants us to use His words to defend against temptation. There have been times when the temptation to sin comes along and I literally can *only* stand up to it by reading Scripture out loud or singing worship songs or quoting a Bible verse I've memorized. Jesus proved that we can win against sin by using words well.

That's pretty awesome.

Talk to God

Dear God, thank You that your words stand up to lies and the temptation to sin. Fill my mind with Your words. Give me discipline to study the Bible and memorize Scripture. Thank You, Jesus, for being my example.

Revolt

Practice memorizing our theme verse, Proverbs 12:18: "Reckless words pierce like a sword, but the tongue of the wise brings healing." If you want to, post our memory verse on your Facebook page or Twitter or make a cool graphic for Instagram or Pinterest. Use the hashtag #SpeakLove at the end of your post. Then we'll all be able to see who is memorizing the Scripture at the same time.

Gossip

Proverbs 11:13

A gossip betrays a confidence, but a trustworthy man keeps a secret.

Somehow, in the modern-girl psyche, there is this belief that if you tell someone all the secrets you know, that makes the two of you closer friends. So instead of keeping the confidences you've promised, you just tell *one* person, because after all, she is your "best friend." Within a matter of days, the secret that only you knew is all over the school or church or Internet. And what you thought would build your "best" friendship has actually just proven that you can't keep your mouth shut.

Exposing weaknesses. Criticizing, teasing, judging in whispers. Gossip tears others down—including you. Here's how gossip tricks us: we think that when we are talking about other people that it makes us closer with the other gossipers. But the real truth? If you are talking behind someone's back with a friend, that friend probably talks behind your back too. Ouch!

I want to be different. Don't you? I mean, I feel the pull as much as you do—to whisper the thing I've heard, to share the scoop. I am not so good at doing the right thing all the time. But I'm trying. I'm wrestling with it. I'm working at it. Wanna join me?

Talk to God

Dear God, I struggle with this. I want to fit in, I want to be in the know because it makes me feel like I have a place. I want to be a good friend; I don't want to be a gossip. But sometimes I don't even realize I'm gossiping. Will you turn on the alerts in my brain? I want to be a good friend whom others can trust.

Revolt

How brave do you feel, my friend? Brave enough to stand up to gossip? I don't want to make you do something that costs you your friends (unless your friends are mean people), but if you hear gossip today, why don't you combat it by saying something nice about the victim of the gossip? Where others are trying to tear down, you toss in a sentence that will build up. Or simply walk away. In time, people will quit gossiping with you and around you. And that will be a good day.

Twitter

Job 33:3

My words come from an upright heart; my lips sincerely speak what I know.

Here we all are on Twitter, with just 140 characters to say something that we hope gets attention. Whether we are trying to be funny, sexy, kind, inspirational, or downright mean, we don't have a lot of space to do it.

So you have to write smartly. Every tweet I send out from @anniedowns takes thought and time. I know that people are reading (even if you only have one follower, someone is reading), and I know I have a chance to use my tweets to bring joy— through laughter or inspiration or whatever.

Twitter is an outlet you have to speak life, to give encouragement, to use your words to help not harm. I've heard terrible stories of teen girls using Twitter to publicly harass other girls, and it makes me sick. We aren't that kind of girls. We are the girls who use every opportunity we can find to give life with our words.

Remember this about Twitter too: once you post something, it's out there forever. The Internet has a weird way of memorizing things. So be wise with your words; be wise with your social media. Every tweet doesn't have to be about Jesus directly—mine aren't. But the goal is to be an encouraging voice in a discouraging world. Twitter is a perfect microphone for that.

Talk to God

Dear God, I want to be an encouraging voice in a discouraging world. Help me to use all my social media outlets to do that. Convict me in the moments when I'm about to use Twitter to hurt and not help. Help me to reflect You in every area of my life.

Revolt

Tweet our memory verse out to your followers (Proverbs 12:18). Use the hashtag #SpeakLove.

Mean Girls

Song of Songs 4:7

All beautiful you are, my darling; there is no flaw in you.

We all know them. For that matter, we've already probably been one, even if just for a minute. A mean girl.

Mean girls say mean things. Mean girls use their words like bullets—they aim for your weakest spot, the place with the least armor, and shoot you. Right there.

I can still easily conjure up memories of rude and unnecessary things that other girls have said to me—about my body, my sports ability, my brain. You name it, the mean girls know how to hurt, don't they?

It reinforces what we already know—words give life or death. I wish I could tell you the magic way to make the words not hurt, or how to make a mean girl stop. But I don't have those answers. Sorry.

Here's what I will tell you: if you are the one being mean, it is absolutely time to stop. Stop being insecure and finding your worth in making others feel bad.[1]

---

1. *My friend Manwell from Group 1 Crew says that mean girls and bullies feel bad about themselves, so they are just looking to make everyone else feel bad too. Sad, but true. If that's you, you are probably awesome; just remember that.*

If you want to combat what the mean girls say (to you or your friends), I do have that trick. Ready? *Speak words of life.* You have the same power—just use it for good! Rescue with your words where other girls have tried to kill. Be encouraging. Be uplifting. Be the voice that heals. (Think about our memory verse, Proverbs 12:18.)

And remember—the mean girls don't win in the end. Jesus wins. Every time.

Talk to God

Dear God, forgive me for the times when I used my tongue to try to hurt someone else. Change my heart. I don't want to be that girl. Give me words to encourage and lift up others. Help me to say the things that heal broken hearts and bring life.

Revolt

Put some good words out there. Post a picture of you and one of your best friends—or even more daring, someone you barely know!—on Instagram and write your favorite thing about her. Use the hashtag #SpeakLove.

Prayer

Matthew 6:9–13

This, then, is how you should pray: "Our Father in heaven, hallowed be your name, your kingdom come, your will be done, on earth as it is in heaven. Give us today our daily bread. Forgive us our debts, as we also have forgiven our debtors. And lead us not into temptation, but deliver us from the evil one."

For some of you, prayer might be a brand-new thing you are just getting into. Others of you have been praying for years. To put it simply, prayer is a conversation between you and God. Jesus made it possible through His sacrificial death, so you could directly connect to a holy, perfect God.

Prayer is a two-way conversation. You can hear God in your heart, but you can also read the Bible since it is full of God's words for you.

Just as you learn and grow through conversations with your friends, the same is true of your relationship with God. The more you talk to Him, the better you get to know Him. And conversations with Him influence all other conversations.

The good news is that Jesus taught us how to pray. It isn't

complicated. And you get better at it the more you practice. Like gymnastics. (I mean, I was always terrible at gymnastics, but I learned how to do a cartwheel and penny-drop into the foam pit—that counts for something, right?) Just start by praying the words Jesus modeled for us to pray. Then add in areas that are important to you—sick relatives, heartache, questions about what to do, thanking Him for all the good things in your life.

There are tons of great verses in the Bible about prayer—use BibleGateway.com to search "pray," "prayer," or "praying."

Talk to God

Dear God, I want to hear You. I want to talk to You. I want prayer to become more important to me every day. Thank You for being a living God who I can talk to. Teach me how to pray.

Revolt

Write out the Lord's Prayer (verses above) in your journal, on your blog, or on note cards to hang in your room. Just put it somewhere and read it over and over. Use this prayer as a guide to get your conversation started.

Today, I wanted to add something extra-special for you, because everyone has moments where it's hard to find the right words to pray. The good news? The Lord's Prayer is not only a great passage to pray directly from the Bible, it can be used as a model that helps you to really connect with God.

I do it a lot to jumpstart my own prayers, either out loud or in my journal. For example:

"Our Father in heaven, hallowed be your name,

I think You're great, God. I worship You. Your name is holy.

your kingdom come, your will be done, on earth as it is in heaven.

Yeah, there are just some things going on, God, that I'm asking for you to step in—like my friend's dad being sick. I pray You would heal him, that Your will would be done. I'm also trying to decide about which project to take next—I want to do whatever is best, whatever is Your will. Will you reveal that to me?

Give us today our daily bread.

It's the end of the month and I'm just not sure I'm going to have enough money, God. But I trust You to provide for me. Please help me to have enough money to get through this last week.

And forgive us our debts, as we also have forgiven our debtors.

Ugh. This is hard for me today because I'm so mad at Susan and how she was talking bad about Karen. I just don't want to be nice to her or be around her. Forgive my hard heart. I know You've forgiven me—help me to forgive her.

And lead us not into temptation, but deliver us from the evil one."

God, it's super hard to stay away from temptation when it is ALL AROUND ME. Would You protect me? Show me the way out of tempting situations and how I can run the other direction.

Now give it a try:

"Our Father in heaven, hallowed be your name,

Lord I Love you and worship You. Help me to show that in my actions, help me to grow in my relationship with you lord Jesus

your kingdom come, your will be done, on earth as it is in heaven.

please watch over Sally Ernst and her family. Her father passed away. Please help them to get through this.

Give us today our daily bread.

Lord help me to do well/better in math and Earth space. Help me prove I can do it. Guide me through this month.

And forgive us our debts, as we also have forgiven our debtors.

Lord help me to forgive Sadie, Harrison and Griffin. Sadie has been very Judgementa and Griffin walked out. Help me to forgiven them $ to be kind to them.

And lead us not into temptation, but deliver us from the evil one."

Lord help me to stay away from temptation. Teach me to go to you and to leave temptation behind.

The Parentals

Deuteronomy 5:16

Honor your father and your mother, as the Lord your God has commanded you, so that you may live long and that it may go well with you in the land the Lord your God is giving you.

Let me first say, I know not everyone has a mom and dad, and that not everyone lives with their mom and dad. And some of you have parents who aren't so awesome. I know. And I'm sorry.

But let me also say this—how you speak to your parents, or the people who are performing the role of parent in your life, says less about who they are and more about what kind of person you are. We aren't here to talk about how your parents act or treat you—we are here to talk about how you should be talking to them.

The Bible makes it clear: Honor your parents. That means speaking with respect and kindness. A college student I know, Kate, does *not* get along with her stepmom. The stepmom isn't super sweet and Kate, to be honest, wasn't so sweet back. But Kate made a choice to speak with kindness, walk away instead of scream in anger, and say one nice thing a day to her stepmom.

And our small group watched as Kate and her stepmom began to get along a little better.

You have to remember this fact: your parents, before they were your parents, were just two humans who, like you, were hurt and healed by words. Even the best parents in the whole world make mistakes. They are often going to act like humans (meaning, not perfect). There are going to be times when their words hurt you and when your words hurt them. But remember who we are—we're the girls starting a word revolution. You can be the one to choose kindness first. Or to hold your tongue when you are angry. See what happens in your home when you watch what you say and choose to create good things with your words.

It could be pretty cool.

Talk to God

Dear God, help me to love and respect my parents. Give me the right words to show them how I feel and how grateful I am for them. Heal their broken places and help us to have a home where we speak life.

Revolt

Just tell your parents thank you today. Tell them how grateful you are for them or for something about them. You could say it in the car on the way to dinner or write it on your Facebook page (because you know your mom is seeing it there—parents love Facebook) or tweet it out to the world.

Pinterest

1 Chronicles 16:8

Give thanks to the Lord, call on his name; make known among the nations what he has done.

I am a big fan of Pinterest. You? Do you love pinning your favorite clothes and recipes and nail art? (Please, people— tell me you appreciate some crazy nail art.) The cool thing about Pinterest is that other people get to see collections of your favorite things and then share it with others.

Just like we talked about with Facebook, Pinterest is a way to use words to share truth with your friends. I have a pin board called "Speak Love Revolution" (http://pinterest.com/annieblogs/speak-love-revolution/) where I pin cool quotes I find— from the Bible, from songs, from movies—that I hope inspire other people.

Pinterest is an easy place to influence others. Especially as we are trying to memorize Proverbs 12:18. I search for that verse to see what kind of cool art people have done with it, and then I pin it to my board. Just another way to share life-giving words.

Talk to God

Dear God, I love the way You show up in our everyday lives. I want to use everything—even my Pinterest boards—to bring You glory and fame. Thanks for the opportunity to use words to show You to the world.

Revolt

Build your own word revolution board. Then as you find awesome quotes, verses, or lyrics from your favorite Christian songs, you can pin them to the board. Use the hashtag #SpeakLove in each pin so that we can search and see them all. (Check that hashtag out—our little gal army is everywhere!)

Journaling

Lamentations 3:22–24

Because of the Lord's great love we are not consumed, for his compassions never fail. They are new every morning; great is your faithfulness. I say to myself, "The Lord is my portion; therefore I will wait for him."

I lead a college small group in Nashville. We spent a lot of time one year talking about the importance of journaling. It grows into a habit after a while, and there are certainly no rules to how, how much, or how often you need to journal. But once you get into journaling, it gives you a place to write down your prayers and questions and day's events and issues and praises.

Did you know the Bible is like a big journal? We can go back to it over and over to read story after story of how God was faithful to His people, how He showed up in their time of need, how He displayed His love.

And that's what your journal can do for you.

I look back on old journals all the time to remind myself of how faithful God has been in my life. I don't journal every day, but I try fairly regularly to write down the things going on in my heart. In some weird way, my own words come back, years later or days later, to encourage me in my walk with God.

You don't have to love writing to be able to journal—and you don't have to write four pages every day! Write a few words. Just a couple sentences of what God is doing. I write out my prayers too, and it's great—because it makes my brain slow down and really process what I am praying. As you journal, you will see that not only will you be able to look back and see what God has done, but you will also remember things to share with others to encourage them.

Talk to God

Dear God, thanks for Your faithfulness in my life. I am grateful for all the ways You have provided for me and cared for me. As I journal about You and our relationship, would You open up the Word to me and help me to know You better?

Revolt

We've included a bunch of journal pages here in *Speak Love Revolution* to help get you going on the discipline of journaling. And whether you are starting new or are already a faithful journal writer, try to write in your journal three days in a row, recording ways that you have seen God's Word impacting each day.

Sounds Good to Me

Proverbs 4:23

Above all else, guard your heart, for everything you do flows from it.

I'm a huge music fan. All types. All the time. In fact, right now bluegrass music is playing through my earbuds. And I'll tell you what I love so much about music—the lyrics. I love what people are able to write—the poetry—that goes with the sounds.

That verse from Proverbs may feel like a weird left turn when we're talking about music, but here's what is true: the lyrics that flow into your ears will find their way to your heart. We need to guard our hearts, so we need to guard our ears.

I'll never be one to tell you to only listen to Christian music, but I will say you should pay close attention to the lyrics you are singing or listening to. If a song talks about self-hate or sex outside of marriage or drug use, why would you listen to those lyrics, ingest those lyrics, repeat those lyrics?

Tons of Christians are making good music—some of it is about Jesus, some isn't. I think of people like Dave Barnes, Matt

Wertz, Drew and Ellie Holcomb, Meredith Andrews, Andrew Ripp, Group 1 Crew, Lecrae, Jake Ousley, Jamie Grace, Steve Moakler, and Ben Rector, just to name a few. Those are the kinds of musicians with lyrics that matter from people who share your faith that should be on repeat in your head.

Fill your heart by filling your ears.

Talk to God

Dear God, thank You for musicians who are pursuing You and growing in their faith. I want to fill my heart with good words and good sounds. Protect me from music that will bring me down and hurt my heart.

Revolt

Share your favorite lyric or your favorite Christian artists with your friends on Facebook, Twitter, Instagram or Pinterest. Use the hashtag #SpeakLove so we can all check out some new music.

Brothers and Sisters

---

1 John 4:20

If anyone says, "I love God," yet hates his brother, he is a liar. For anyone who does not love his brother, whom he has seen, cannot love God, whom he has not seen.

When I was in middle school, my mom made me write this verse one hundred times. She swears she doesn't remember it. But trust me, I'm the one who sat at my desk in my bedroom, mad as a wet hen, and wrote "if if if … anyone anyone anyone … says says says …" for hours. I mean, *hours.*

I wasn't nice to my little sisters. I said mean things. Because of my hurts, I hurt them. And I was a Christian the whole time. So Mom decided to use words to teach me how to better use mine. So over and over I wrote this verse and began to actually understand it. *Huh! I do say I love God, and I do treat my sisters terribly—how does that work? How can that be?*

Sometimes the hardest mission field is the one in your own home, isn't it? I know, I know. Little brothers can be annoying. Older sisters can be rude (ahem, I was). Little sisters seem to always be underfoot and big brothers are perfect. (At least, that's what I always imagined.) No matter where you fall in the sibling line of your family, you have the chance to bring this word revolution to your house.

Talk to God

Dear God, thank You for my siblings. Thanks for putting us in the same family. Even on the days when they make me crazy, I'm glad that someone else knows what it is like to grow up in our home. Help me to use my words to bring life, joy, and healing to our home. Help us to be a team who works together.

Revolt

Whether you have one brother or ten sisters, write something nice about each sibling on his or her Facebook wall or write a kind tweet about each of them. Use the hashtag #SpeakLove.

Dudes

Proverbs 16:24

Gracious words are a honeycomb, sweet to the soul and healing to the bones.

Boys are awesome. They are. Maybe not perfect, but neither are we, right?

How you speak to the guys in your life—from your dad to your bros to your friends and the boys you like (and used to like)—really matters.

My friends and I used to complain a lot about the boys here in Nashville. I don't really know how it started, but it got to be a habit. Frustrated, someone would say, "Uh, Nashville boys," and all the girls would roll their eyes.

What were we creating with our words? Nothing good, that's for sure.

So we made a decision. About twenty of us. No more talking about dudes like that. So we stopped. We decided instead that we were going to build them up with our words.

You should try it. When the opportunity to complain about a guy—whether it is your dad or your boyfriend or your youth pastor or that guy who sits by you in class—choose instead to say something good about him. Guys have a lot of struggles (so do we, I know), but wouldn't you like to be known for the gal who cheers for the guys in her life, not the one who tears them down?

Talk to God

Dear God, thanks for making men and women. I pray for opportunities to speak life and love to the men I know. Give me the right words, with the right boundaries, to encourage the guys in my life.

Revolt

Why not encourage your dad today? Or maybe encourage one of your guy friends. Which guy in your life could use a kind word? Give it!

Worship

John 4:24

"God is spirit, and his worshipers must worship in spirit and in truth."

Every time you speak, you are creating something—remember Proverbs 18:21? So when you worship, you are creating the most beautiful of things.

Worship is the best use of your words when it comes to music. Singing to God, singing about God, singing with others who believe what we believe. There is such power in worshiping with other believers—even if it is just the people on the other side of the speakers.

(Yes, worship is a lifestyle—not just what you sing—but, you know, we're starting a word revolution, so we're gonna focus on the word stuff. Cool?)

There are tons of great worship albums. Some of you may love hymns (I do) or modern worship that my grandfather says sounds like "a rock concert" (I love that too). My all-time favorite is "Cutting Edge" by Delirious?.[1] Check with your youth

---

1. *If you are looking for some other worship artists, check out Hillsong United, Kari Jobe, Kim Walker, Bethel Live, David Crowder, Chris Tomlin, Matt Redman, and Cory Asbury, just to name a few.*

minister, small group leader, parents, or other Christians to see what worship albums they love.

There's this amazing thing about worship too—when we worship God, telling Him how great He is and singing about life with Him, He comes and blesses us. Seems backward, doesn't it? But that is how it works.

Talk to God

Dear God, You are so worthy to be worshiped in spirit and in truth. Help me to make worshiping with music a daily part of my life. I want my whole life to be worship to You. Use my words to worship You.

Revolt

Share a link to your favorite worship song (from YouTube or Vimeo) with your friends on Facebook, Twitter, or Pinterest. Use the hashtag #SpeakLove.

Half Way!

Congrats, friend! You are halfway through *Speak Love Revolution*! Is your life different? Are you loving your friends better? Journaling more? Speaking kindly to your parents?

I wonder if you are struggling. I bet you are. I am. As I am writing this, I am fighting against the temptations to use my words in all the wrong ways. It seems that when we are focused on being more like Jesus in any area, that same area has so many pressures, doesn't it?

Don't quit. We are changing things. We are using life-giving words to change our own hearts and the hearts of those around us.

Press on, sister. It will be worth it.

Lying

Colossians 3:8–10

But now you must also rid yourselves of all such things as these: anger, rage, malice, slander, and filthy language from your lips. Do not lie to each other, since you have taken off your old self with its practices and have put on the new self, which is being renewed in knowledge in the image of its Creator.

I always want to tell a good story. It's in my bones. When I was younger, I would tell the best story I could think up—even if it was only partially true. When I lied about something, I always felt guilty. But I wanted to fit in, be popular, and be loved more than I wanted to be honest. Yuck.

I was growing a garden of weeds with my lying tongue. Speaking truth, telling the true story, grows beautiful flowers of life. It all goes back to the same thing, my friend—what you are creating with your words.

You have to choose the honest way, the way of highest integrity. It's more than the words you say; it is who you are. Jesus said that He is the way and the *truth* and the life. That same Jesus is the one you, as a Christian, asked to live in you. So you are already full of truth. Make sure your words reflect that.

I know it can be hard. But remember that your words are all about growing and creating something. This is your chance to change the past and become a girl who is known for her honest words.

Talk to God

Dear God, I want to radiate truth. I want the words of my mouth to flow with honesty. I want people around me to see You in the things I say. Forgive me for the times when lying was easier and I gave in to it. Strengthen me. Grow me.

Revolt

This one is easy, my friend. Just tell the truth today. Every time you get the chance.

Celebrities

Proverbs 21:1

In the Lord's hand the king's heart is a stream of water that he channels toward all who please him.

I think this may be my favorite day of the word revolution, and I'll tell you why: We have no idea when God is working in someone else's heart and life, and as the verse says above God holds hearts and turns them. The loudest voices in our culture are the celebrities—what if they just need to know someone is praying for them?

A few weeks ago, I saw a segment on a late-night television show where celebrities read tweets that other people had written about them. All the tweets were mean. It was funny to watch— you know, an actress reading how someone thinks she is "overrated"—but it was also really sad. I think we forget that they are real people too. And words affect them.

What if God is already working on their heart and your tweet saying something kind draws them closer to Him?

Your words matter. Your words matter. Your words matter.

For those people in the world who hear praises like "I love

you so much" from strangers and curses like "You are the worst actor ever" from strangers, we can be different.

What if God used *you* to encourage an influential voice in our culture? That's a word revolution, my friend.

Talk to God

Dear God, I pray today for the people in our culture who have so many eyes on them. Be near to them. Draw them to You. Give the Christians in Hollywood a voice to speak out their beliefs. Bless those who share their art with us. Show me who I should encourage—make it clear. And use the words I say to bring life to them.

Revolt

You probably see this one coming. Pick one or two of your favorite celebrities. Find them on Facebook or Twitter or Instagram and send an encouraging message. Share your favorite verse, pray for them, and tell them that you are praying for them. Thank them for sharing their talents with the world. Probably don't say "I love you so much" because, well, you don't really know them. Use the hashtag #SpeakLove so that we can see lots of famous people be encouraged by these gals on a word revolution. (It's gonna be fun, huh?)

Enemies & Frenemies

Matthew 5:43–44

"You have heard that it was said, 'Love your neighbor and hate your enemy.' But I tell you, love your enemies and pray for those who persecute you."

I have some bad news for you. Someone somewhere probably doesn't like you. I know. I hate hearing it too. For my serious people-pleaser streak, this is bad, bad news.

But you know what? It's okay. Really. You are going to interact with people your whole life who think you are awesome and with people who think you are less than awesome. The truth of the matter is that how others treat you should not decide who you are or how you act. So even if you have to spend time in the same classroom as that mean girl *every day*, or deal with your brother being a punk, or hear "friends" say ugly things about you, the Bible tells us exactly what to do. Love and pray for them anyway.

Which is really easy.

Yeah, right.

I don't know that I have enemies, but I can think of two people whom I really don't care for—they each have either hurt me directly or hurt people I care dearly about. So trust me, I struggle with how to pray for people like that and how to forgive and how to love them. But I have to—I at least have to struggle through it and fight every day to be a part of the word revolution. I pray you fight that urge too—the urge to be ugly back, to tear down with words, even when it seems deserving.

Love your enemies. Jesus did. It's how the world will know that we are different—by our love (see John 13:35).

Talk to God

Dear God, it is hard, hard, hard to love people who treat me unkindly and feel like my enemies. I don't know how to do it. I really don't. Change my heart, and my words, so that I can reflect You to the world.

Revolt

Sister, hold your tongue in the moment. That's the best revolt. Silence. Don't fight back; don't gossip. I encourage you to even say one nice thing about the person who is your enemy (or frenemy). And pray. For them. For yourself. For reconciliation and forgiveness. For words of life to infuse the situation and, like a tea bag in a cup of water, change the flavor of the relationship.

Cussing

Ephesians 4:29

Do not let any unwholesome talk come out of your mouths, but only what is helpful for building others up according to their needs, that it may benefit those who listen.

Cussing is this thing that just sorta falls into your vocabulary over time, isn't it? I remember hearing my friends in elementary school say words that, honestly, I didn't know. I was—and still am—an avid reader, and so it surprised me when they were using descriptive words I had never heard. (I know. Such an innocent little lamb.)

I wish I never felt the need to be cool and integrate any of those words—from the mildest to the perceived big ones—into my vocabulary because I wanted to be cool. But I did. And they were in the music I listened to and the movies I watched.

I know the arguments: *Who decides what words are cuss words? Why is it such a big deal? These weren't cuss words one hundred years ago … yada, yada, yada.* But here is the truth. If you are a part of this word revolution, and you want to speak life instead of death, cuss words don't need to be a part of your vocabulary. They just don't.

They bring you down. They bring down the people around you. While we are all allowed to make mistakes, when you are trying to live a godly example in front of your friends, removing cuss words is an easy way to eliminate a stumbling block for others. You can get the same point across, no matter what you are trying to say, without using foul language. I promise, you can.

Talk to God

Dear God, please raise my sensitivity. I don't want to think cuss words or hear cuss words and not be taken aback a little. Help me to clean up my language—convict me when I'm about to speak words that aren't bringing life.

Revolt

Try this experiment. Every time you feel inclined to cuss, replace it with an audible "BEEP." Every time. It won't take long until you're beeping less and are able to remove those foul words from your vocab all together. Revolt against the notion that cussing is cool. It's not.

The Gospel

1 Peter 3:15

But in your hearts revere Christ as Lord. Always be prepared to give an answer to everyone who asks you to give the reason for the hope that you have. But do this with gentleness and respect.

You know what one of the absolute joys of our faith is? Telling others about it. It doesn't have to be scary; it doesn't have to be intimidating. In fact, it can mainly just be great—because you are sharing about a relationship. You are telling others about someone you love, someone who loves you, and someone who gave His life for you *and* for everyone.

I used to get so intimidated at the idea of "sharing the Gospel." (Say that in a deep, manly voice, like I just did, and you'll know what I mean.) But I have learned that what draws a lot of people to deeper faith or a new faith walk with Jesus is hearing stories of how real Jesus is in my life. I don't have to have Scriptures memorized (though I should!) and I don't have to follow some perfect script about Jesus. I just have to be prepared to give an answer for the hope that I have.

Jesus gives me lots of hope, y'all. Without Him, I would be

an absolute mess. I like to say, "Jesus saved me once, but He rescues me all the time"—and it is true. So when I am hanging around with my non-Christian friends, I don't have a pamphlet on Christianity and I don't go through the Roman Road. (Google that—it's actually really cool and a great way to share about Jesus's sacrifice and resurrection.) I just like to talk about what God is doing in my life, why I chose to be a Christian in the first place, and how that relationship has shaped my life.

Don't be scared. You can't save anybody—that's Jesus's job. Just talk about Him.

Talk to God

Dear God, open my eyes to the friends around me who do not know You. Give me the right words to say. Give me the courage and the opportunity to share about what Jesus did for us all. I pray that my words will not only be life-giving, but encourage someone else to make eternal life choices.

Revolt

Today, bring Jesus up in a conversation with someone who does not know Him. Then journal about the experience and pray for that friend.

Talking to Others about Jesus

Presenting the entire Gospel to someone can feel scary—I understand. But my friend Chris Wheeler came up with this amazing way of presenting what everyone needs to know that is not only easy to remember, it shows just how true and real everything is. With his permission, I want to share his ten sentences on the Gospel here so you can use them if you get the chance:

THE GOSPEL IN TEN SENTENCES

1. God is **HOLY.**

2. God **created** the world. (Genesis 1:1)

3. God **created humankind** for His Glory. (Genesis 1:26–27)

4. Humanity **sinned** against God and now all are born sinners. (Romans 3:23)

5. Sin **separates** humanity from God who is HOLY. (John 3:3)

6. Sin **deserves** death and eternal separation from God. (Romans 6:23)

7. Jesus is both **God & Man** … God's son came to earth as a man & lived a sinless life.

8. Jesus **took our punishment** for our sins by dying on the cross. (Romans 5:8, John 3:16, 1 Peter 3:18)

9. Jesus **came back to life** three days later … He beat death!

10. Jesus offers forgiveness for our sin as a **free gift** to all who would repent & believe. (1 John 1:9, John 14:6, John 5:24, John 10:10, Romans 10:9–11)

Facebook / Instagram / Tumblr

Matthew 5:14–16

"You are the light of the world. A city on a hill cannot be hidden. Neither do people light a lamp and put it under a bowl. Instead they put it on its stand, and it gives light to everyone in the house. In the same way, let your light shine before men, that they may see your good deeds and praise your Father in heaven."

I really like Facebook. I love getting to keep up with my friends and seeing pictures of their lives. In 2011, Mark Zuckerberg (the founder of Facebook) reported that one in every nine people on Earth has a Facebook account. If your friend group is anything like mine, it's more like eight out of nine (including my mom).

You know what is cool about Facebook, and other social media like Instagram and Tumblr? They give us an outlet, every day, to say whatever we want to the people who are our friends. It's exactly what girls like us want—a way to share life-giving words. A way to start this word revolution. I have a friend in Scotland who, almost every day, says something on Facebook about what God is doing in her life. It's not every post, and it's not annoying; it's just her real experience. I like that. It encourages me.

One of my favorite things about Instagram is creating word art of verses or quotes and posting them. I also like taking a picture with my friends and posting it, so that my friends know how grateful I am for them! As in all cases, Instagram can be a mean and ugly place, but we are there to bring light! So we post things that encourage others, not intentionally make them feel left out. We use our artistic sides to create posts on Tumblr or Instragram that are life-giving.

(P. S.: You know what is REALLY fun? When we get to use something that wasn't meant to make God more famous—like Facebook or Tumblr or Instagram—and use it to bring Him fame. That's pretty rad.)

Talk to God

Dear God, thank You for my friends. Thanks for connections and the opportunity to use social media to bring You glory. Help me to see how I can use my time on each of these outlets to encourage others and help people see You. I am Yours, my whole life—including my Facebook page, Instagram feed, and Tumblr.

Revolt

Encourage your friends to join this word revolution. Here's a status update that you can post: Hey girls! Join me in the Speak Love Revolution—30 Days to Change Our World! #SpeakLove

Trash In, Trash Out

Luke 6:45

The good man brings good things out of the good stored up in his heart, and the evil man brings evil things out of the evil stored up in his heart. For out of the overflow of his heart his mouth speaks.

When I was in college, I listened to a variety of music. Most of the songs I enjoyed were fine, but a few (truthfully, a few of my favorites) had more than one cuss word in them. I thought it was no big deal to listen to them once in a while … or once in a week … or once in a day.

One night, my roommates and I sat down to dinner in our apartment. I honestly don't even remember what we were talking about, but all of a sudden, when I went to say something, I said the f-word. The big one. They stopped talking and eating and stared at me. Then they turned pale, and their eyes bugged out. But so did mine. I had never intended to say that; it just came out. The moment that word shot out of my mouth, I knew exactly which song had put it in my head. I jumped out of my chair, ran to my room, and deleted that music immediately.

Seriously, I did. Then I returned to the table and continued to eat dinner, totally embarrassed.

You know what went wrong here? I had allowed all sorts of rubbish in and that is what came out. I'm not going to give you rules on what kind of things you should listen to, read, or watch. I'm simply going to tell you this truth: what you let into your mind fills your heart. What fills your heart comes out of your mouth. Just pay attention; you'll see that you are more inclined to cuss when you hear it and more likely to be disrespectful when that is what you see in movies. It's weird but true.

Again, no rules here. I just want to encourage you to guard your heart and mind so that the words that come out of your mouth are like a river of crystal clear water. No trash.

Talk to God

Dear God, I want to glorify You by guarding what I let in. Open my eyes to entertainment that is uplifting and edifying. Raise my sensitivity to things that lead to words of death.

Revolt

For the next seven days (the rest of this devotional), go on a trash fast. Take a break from TV and movies, step away from ungodly music. Focus on books about God and your relationship with Him. Listen to music that glorifies God. After seven days of this trash fast, you'll be surprised at how you don't miss it, how foul language shocks you, and realize how much better life is when you are filling your mind with good things.

Read On, Reader

---

2 Timothy 3:16–17

All Scripture is God-breathed and is useful for teaching, rebuking, correcting and training in righteousness, so that the man of God may be thoroughly equipped for every good work.

I am a pure book nerd. From childhood when I used to read in the bathtub (and drop books in the water all the time) to now as an adult when I usually would rather read than do almost anything else, books have been my constant companion.

I became a Christian when I was five, so the Bible has always been a part of my reading life. But I haven't always enjoyed it. To be honest, parts of it are just plain boring—lists, laws, and things that my brain doesn't quite understand. As I have matured in my faith, I have grown to see the Bible for what it really is—not some boring old book that Christians have to read, but a collection of stories, lessons, and love from God to us. I love reading it. In fact, I have a reading plan where I try to read the Bible in a year. I'm on my second round, and it's going fine so far.

Lots of great Christian books are out there—authors who love God and are working hard to write things that are interesting and entertaining and meaningful for you in your walk with Christ. I think of people like Emily Freeman, Ann Voskamp, Tricia Goyer, Sandra Byrd, Shannon Primicerio, Mary DeMuth, Catherine Marshall, Elizabeth Elliot—women who have used or are using their gifts to give us books to read, both fiction and nonfiction, that teach us about Jesus.

These are the exact kinds of things we should be putting into our minds to make sure that the words that flow from our hearts to our mouths are life-giving.

Talk to God

Dear God, thank You for Your Word and how the Bible is living and active and is real in our world today. Increase my love for the Bible, my desire to read it, and give me a heart that loves to study Your Word.

Revolt

What is your favorite book by a Christian author? Share that title and author on your Facebook page or on mine (Facebook.com/annieblogs)! Make sure to use the hashtag #SpeakLove so we can all check out the new, awesome books out there.

Write for God

Revelation 12:11

They overcame him by the blood of the Lamb and by the word of their testimony; they did not love their lives so much as to shrink from death.

The "him" mentioned above is the same "him" from Day 2—that nasty serpent, the devil. I love this verse because it reminds us that we are already victorious—we have everything we need to defeat the enemy in our lives.

You were saved by the blood of the Lamb (Jesus), and the word of your testimony overcomes the enemy and his temptations. That's why I do what I do, y'all. I spend my life writing out stories of God's faithfulness, daily testimonies, so that the enemy doesn't win in my life and so others can be encouraged by the way God moves in me.

He does the same for you, you know. He is always working on your behalf. Sometimes you just have to look around to see it. You may not be a natural-born writer—that's fine. You may not enjoy writing at all—that's cool. (We can still be friends.) But at certain times in your life, doors may open for you to write about

God. Take those chances! We overcome the enemy by the words of our testimony.

If you love to write, my friend, write on. Write every day. Whether it is a status update, a blog, or a book, pour your heart into words and then share some of them with the world.

Think of all the books you've read after which you could say, "Wow, that book changed my life." It was the power of words. The power of someone else sharing their testimony. And now it is your turn. Share, share, share. Write of His love, write of His faithfulness. We all have stories to tell—every single one of us. Tell yours. For the glory of God.

Talk to God

Dear God, use my words to bring You glory. Whether they are in my journal, in notes to others, online, in a school newspaper, or on a bookstore shelf, use my words to draw people closer to You.

Revolt

Whether you love to write or not, you should write down your testimony—the story of when and why you decided to accept Jesus to be your Lord and Savior. You don't have to have a crazy testimony (I don't) to have a story that God can use to draw people to Himself. You never know when you are going to get the chance to share that, and it is powerful!

Just a Quick Note

Proverbs 25:11

A word aptly spoken is like apples of gold in settings of silver.

Don't you love snail mail? As much as email and texting is certainly faster and easier, there is something beautiful about a handwritten note.

Before my small group girls went home for the summer, we each wrote our addresses on five envelopes. Then we traded envelopes, and everyone left with five letters to write and mail. Throughout the summer, I would go to my P.O. Box with my fingers crossed that there would be a note from one of the girls in there.

There is something really powerful about kind words written down for a friend. As the verse says, when you use your words well, they are priceless to those who receive them.

You can save notes like that, the ones that people mail you for encouragement. In fact, throughout my journals over the years, I have taped notes that have spoken to my heart.

It doesn't take a lot of time, but a handwritten note is a gift that can impact someone forever. Don't take this day lightly—a few minutes prayerfully hovering over a note that you mail to a friend could bless her and change her life in ways you don't know. Words create life, remember?

This is your moment, sister. Write a note. Share life. Give encouragement. Mail the gift of words to people who may need it more than you could ever imagine.

Talk to God

Dear God, bring to mind all the right people who need an encouraging note today. Lead me to the right verses to share and the best words that will bring life. May these notes that go out honor You and bring You glory.

Revolt

Stop by the store and get a stack of cards from the stationery section. Buy some stamps, ask some of your friends for their home addresses, grab your favorite pen, and send out some notes. Share your favorite Bible verse or one that means a lot to you right now. Encourage your friends by talking about the favorite qualities you see in them. Then put a stamp on it and mail that puppy.

(You know, call me crazy, but you could mail notes to your family—yes, the ones who live in your house—if you wanted to. Or your small group, Young Life, or youth leader. Adults need encouragement too!)

So send out five notes, snail-mail style, to people you care about.

Praying for Others

Philippians 1:3–6

I thank my God every time I remember you. In all my prayers for all of you, I always pray with joy because of your partnership in the gospel from the first day until now, being confident of this, that he who began a good work in you will carry it on to completion until the day of Christ Jesus.

I think I don't know how powerful prayer really is. I mean, I pray for my friends and I have definitely seen God move in their lives, but sometimes I forget that prayer is a tool God has given us to directly affect the world.

I hope you pray for your friends. I hope you pray for your family. But I know firsthand that sometimes it's hard to remember all the people we need to pray for. My friend Katie taught me a cool trick a few years ago: I have seven note cards, each with a different topic written on it (family, friends, future, my church, the world, etc.), and on them I keep a running list of important prayer requests or needs. I also put stars beside my prayers that God has answered. With these cards, I flip through them daily and pray for a few minutes over each of them.

Praying for others takes the focus off of you. If you just pray for yourself and your own needs all day every day, that will lead to a pretty selfish lifestyle. It does good things for your insides to take words of prayer and turn them toward other people.

Pray for your people. Take them before God, and ask Him to move on their behalf.

Talk to God

Dear God, I am grateful for the people You have placed in my life. Give me a heart that loves to pray—especially for others. Open my eyes to the prayer needs of those around me. Teach me how to pray for my friends and family members.

Revolt

Make a list of five people at the end of this devotion that you can commit to pray for, using the lines below. It can be family or friends or whomever you want—just pick five and pray for them every day this week. Ask God to bless them, and pray for their needs (you could even ask them if they have anything they want you to pray about). If they don't know Jesus, pray for their salvation.[1] The Bible says to watch and pray—do it and watch God move.

---

1. You could also make note cards like I've done—it has helped my prayer life SO much!

Five people I can pray for:

_____

_____

_____

_____

_____

What God Says About You

---

1 Peter 2:9

But you are a chosen people, a royal priesthood, a holy nation, God's special possession, that you may declare the praises of him who called you out of darkness into his wonderful light.

Here's another truth for your truth basket. (I don't know what makes me think you have a truth basket, but let's just go with it.) The reason we are able to use words to encourage and speak life into others is because God is always encouraging us and speaking life into us—if we are listening.

This is beautiful reason to spend time reading and studying the Bible. It is full of verses meant to affirm who *you* are. Throughout the Scriptures, God has written out words about each of us—like the verse above—that you can cling to.

When I need to be reminded that God loves me, there is verse after verse, like Psalm 100:5, to tell me that. When I need to be reminded that God has a plan for my life, I just have to flip to Jeremiah 29:11.

When I forget that I am forgiven, I go back and read Psalm 103:11–12 and am reminded of how God has removed my sin as far as the east is from the west (that's far, y'all).

You see, He knows the power of words because He created the world with them. When God speaks words of life over us, it changes who we are. And then, in turn, we get to pour words of life over our friends, family, *and* people who don't know Jesus.

Read what God says about you. Digest His words. Believe them. Enjoy them. And know that they are for you.

Talk to God

Dear God, thank You for filling the Bible with verses about who I am in Christ. I want Your love for me to be my whole identity. Do that in me. Open the Bible to me so I can see the verses that tell of Your love for me.

Revolt

Post Jeremiah 29:11 on Instagram, your Facebook page, Twitter, or add it to your Speak Love Revolution Pinterest board. Hashtag it #SpeakLove.

Words Lead to Actions

1 John 3:18

Dear children, let us not love with words or speech but with actions and in truth.

I used to teach elementary school, and each year for the first few days all I did was teach the classroom rules to all the students.[1] We would practice walking in line, how to go through the cafeteria to get lunch, and how the overall rules worked.

My words would instruct them and they would act in response to that. That is the definition of obedience.

You already know by now that your words have power and can create life or death. The other thing your words can do? Cause action. What you say can lead others to act.

I mean, take this whole devotional for example. Here I am, sitting in a hotel room in Charlotte, North Carolina, writing about the power of words. And there you are, wherever you are, responding to those words.

Words lead to actions.

---

1. *You remember those first days of each new school year from your childhood, don't you?*

If you tell yourself over and over how ugly you are, your actions will reflect that. If you keep speaking life over your little sister, she will act in confidence. That's why it is important to use your words well; they are going to lead to action, in your own life or in someone else's.

Your words, my friend, are so powerful. Please, don't forget that.

Talk to God

Dear God, as I seek to live and use my words to glorify You, help me to remember the power of what I say. When I speak to others, and when I talk about myself, I want those words to lead to actions that further Your kingdom.

Revolt

Ask one or two friends to buy or download *The Speak Love Revolution*, then meet together to take action. Pray for each other, mail cards to some of their friends or family, brainstorm how you each can share words of encouragement at home, etc. Get ready to act.

Memorize

Psalm 119:105

Your word is a lamp to my feet and a light for my path.

We are twenty-nine days in! I am so hoping that you already have Proverbs 12:18 memorized. If not, you better get to practicing, sister!

The first verses I remember memorizing came thanks to some kids' music. The tapes (yes, cassette tapes—google it if I lost you) were called GT & the Halo Express, and each song taught me a different verse. I lost those tapes years and years ago, but last year for Christmas (as an adult, by the way) I got the entire CD set of those songs. And I still listen to and still love them, thank you very much.

Here's the thing about memorizing Scripture—no matter where you are, if you know verses by heart they will encourage and uplift you. For the things you struggle with the most, memorize Scripture to fight off those temptations. The verses that speak to you of God's love and His heart for you—if you have those locked away in your brain, you always know them.

How do you decide what to memorize? Start with verses that you love. You could also choose verses your pastor or your youth minister uses. Pull up BibleGateway.com to find verses that are topical, like if you want to memorize Scripture about God's love. Or you could go back and memorize some of the verses in *The Speak Love Revolution*.

Hide His Word in your heart. It will change everything.

Talk to God

Dear God, I want to hide Your Word in my heart. It isn't easy memorizing Scripture, but I want to do it. Please open my mind to be capable to latch onto these words. Lead me to the Scriptures that are on Your heart for me to memorize.

Revolt

Write out our memory verse (Proverbs 12:18) *without* looking. Post it on Facebook, Twitter, Instagram or Pinterest. Use the hashtag #SpeakLove and then you'll be able to see all the other gals around the world who are memorizing the same Scriptures as you.

Welsh Revival

1 Peter 1:8–9

Though you have not seen him, you love him; and even though you do not see him now, you believe in him and are filled with an inexpressible and glorious joy, for you are receiving the end result of your faith, the salvation of your souls.

You wanna hear about a serious word revolution? You want to hear how one teenage girl changed everything with one sentence?

Then read about the start of the Welsh Revival in 1904[1]:

In February 1904, the Spirit of God bade [Pastor Jenkins] introduce some new feature into the young people's meeting held after the morning service, and it dawned on him to ask for testimony, *definite testimony*, as to what the Lord had done for their own souls.

---

1. This excerpt comes from *The Awakening in Wales: A First-hand Account of the Welsh Revival of 1904* by Jessie Penn-Lewis, CLC Publications (Fort Washington, PA), 1993, 2012, pp. 61-62.

One or two rose to speak, but it was not testimony. It was just then that the same young girl [named Florrie Evans, who had been afraid to give her life to Christ the night before]—shy, nervous, intelligent—stood up in tears and with clasped hands simply said with a deep pathos, "Oh I love Jesus Christ with all my heart." Instantly, the Spirit of God appears to have fallen upon the gathering … It was the beginning of the visible manifestation of the Spirit breaking out in life.

Several reports say that this confession was what set the church on fire for God. Can you dig that? One teen girl. *One sentence* about Jesus. And it sparked a revival in the whole country.

Those are some powerful words.

I chose this to be our last day together on purpose. Because from the day I heard this story, it has not stopped rocking my world. The idea that a teenage girl being brave enough to say that one sentence—"I love the Lord Jesus with all my heart"—could change an entire country has me absolutely fired up.

That could be you.

Those words gave life and life to the full, didn't they?

So as we part ways, I hope you read 1 Peter 1:8–9 again. I hope you memorize it. I hope that you live it every day.

Even though you have not seen Jesus, you love Him.

And even though you don't see Him now, you believe and are filled with joy.

Tell somebody.

Your words matter. Use them.

Talk to God

Dear God, at the end of this word revolution, I just want You to know that I don't want to be the same anymore—I don't want to be the girl who started this thirty days ago. I want to be a revolutionary. I want to change the world with my words. Open doors. Show me how. Let me reflect You with my words.

Revolt

Post Florrie's proclamation, if it is true for you, on Facebook, Twitter, Instagram, or whatever social networks you use. Use the hashtag #SpeakLove.

What's Next?

What now? That's a great question, and I think you are the best one to answer it.

How is your life different? How has this thirty-day word revolution changed the way you write, speak, type, and even think? What has God done in your heart?

Journal about it if you haven't been journaling all along. Write about the result of the time you poured into this study.

Dear friend, well done. We have revolted together and changed something in the world. And it is going to keep getting bigger.

Want to keep going with the word revolution? Get a bunch of your friends to buy or download it, and go through it again—this time you lead the group. Keep checking into the #SpeakLove hashtag and comment on what other girls around the world are saying about changing the way we Christian women use words.

This has been so fun, y'all. So, so fun. I hope it is just the beginning of some amazing things God is going to do in our lives.

Thanks for walking with me through this. I'd love to hear about your experience. Will you pop over to my Facebook page (Facebook.com/annieblogs) and let me know? I want to hear what God is doing in your life!

Just remember—your words matter. Every day.

To God be the glory!

Sincerely,

Annie

Reckless words pierce like a sword, but the tongue of the wise brings healing.

Proverbs 12:18

_____

_____

_____

_____

_____

_____

_____

_____

_____

_____

_____

_____

_____

_____

The tongue has the power of life and death, and those who love it will eat its fruit.

Proverbs 18:21

_May the words of my mouth and the meditation of my heart
be pleasing in your sight, O Lord, my Rock, and my Redeemer._

Psalm 19:14

A gossip betrays a confidence, but a trustworthy man keeps a secret.

Proverbs 11:13

I have hidden your word in my heart that I might not sin against you.

Psalm 119:11

_____

_____

_____

_____

_____

_____

_____

_____

_____

_____

_____

_____

_____

Give thanks to the Lord, call on his name; make known among the nations what he has done.

1 Chronicles 16:8

_____

_____

_____

_____

_____

_____

_____

_____

_____

_____

_____

_____

_____

_____

_____

Above all else, guard your heart, for it is the wellspring of life.

Proverbs 4:23

A word aptly spoken is like apples of gold in settings of silver.

Proverbs 25:11

Your word is a lamp to my feet and a light for my path.

Psalm 119:105

_____

_____

_____

_____

_____

_____

_____

_____

_____

_____

_____

_____

_____

Pleasant words are a honeycomb, sweet to the soul and healing to the bones.

Proverbs 16:24

_____

_____

_____

_____

_____

_____

_____

_____

_____

_____

_____

_____

_____

God is spirit, and his worshipers must worship in spirit and in truth.

John 4:24

_____

_____

_____

_____

_____

_____

_____

_____

_____

_____

_____

_____

The king's heart is in the hand of the Lord; he directs it like a watercourse wherever he pleases.

Proverbs 21:1

By this all men will know that you are my disciples, if you love one another.

John 13:35

_____

_____

_____

_____

_____

_____

_____

_____

_____

_____

_____

_____

_____

Do not let any unwholesome talk come out of your mouths, but only what is helpful for building others up according to their needs, that it may benefit those who listen.

Ephesians 4:29

But in your hearts set apart Christ as Lord. Always be prepared to give an answer to everyone who asks you to give the reason for the hope that you have.

1 Peter 3:15

_____

_____

_____

_____

_____

_____

_____

_____

_____

_____

_____

_____

_____

_____

_____

_____

You brood of vipers, how can you who are evil say anything good? For out of the overflow of the heart the mouth speaks.

Matthew 12:34

My words come from an upright heart; my lips sincerely speak what I know.

Job 33:3

_____

_____

_____

_____

_____

_____

_____

_____

_____

_____

_____

_____

_____

_____

_____

_____

_____

_____

Reckless words pierce like a sword, but the tongue of the wise brings healing.

Proverbs 12:18

_____

_____

_____

_____

_____

_____

_____

_____

_____

_____

_____

_____

_____

_____

The tongue has the power of life and death, and those who love it will eat its fruit.

Proverbs 18:21

_____

_____

_____

_____

_____

_____

_____

_____

_____

_____

_____

_____

_____

*May the words of my mouth and the meditation of my heart
be pleasing in your sight, O Lord, my Rock, and my Redeemer.*

Psalm 19:14

A gossip betrays a confidence, but a trustworthy man keeps a secret.

Proverbs 11:13

_____

_____

_____

_____

_____

_____

_____

_____

_____

_____

_____

_____

_____

I have hidden your word in my heart that I might not sin against you.

Psalm 119:11

Give thanks to the Lord, call on his name; make known among the nations what he has done.

1 Chronicles 16:8

Above all else, guard your heart, for it is the wellspring of life.

Proverbs 4:23

A word aptly spoken is like apples of gold in settings of silver.

Proverbs 25:11

_____

_____

_____

_____

_____

_____

_____

_____

_____

_____

_____

_____

_____

Your word is a lamp to my feet and a light for my path.

Psalm 119:105

_____

_____

_____

_____

_____

_____

_____

_____

_____

_____

_____

_____

_____

_____

_____

_____

_____

Pleasant words are a honeycomb, sweet to the soul and healing to the bones.

Proverbs 16:24

_____

_____

_____

_____

_____

_____

_____

_____

_____

_____

_____

_____

_____

God is spirit, and his worshipers must worship in spirit and in truth.

John 4:24

_____

_____

_____

_____

_____

_____

_____

_____

_____

_____

_____

_____

_____

_____

_____

The king's heart is in the hand of the Lord; he directs it like a watercourse wherever he pleases.

Proverbs 21:1

By this all men will know that you are my disciples, if you love one another.

John 13:35

_____

_____

_____

_____

_____

_____

_____

_____

_____

_____

_____

_____

_____

Do not let any unwholesome talk come out of your mouths, but only what is helpful for building others up according to their needs, that it may benefit those who listen.

Ephesians 4:29

_____

_____

_____

_____

_____

_____

_____

_____

_____

_____

_____

_____

_____

_____

_____

_____

_____

_____

But in your hearts set apart Christ as Lord. Always be prepared to give an answer to everyone who asks you to give the reason for the hope that you have.

1 Peter 3:15

You brood of vipers, how can you who are evil say anything good? For out of the overflow of the heart the mouth speaks.

Matthew 12:34

_____

_____

_____

_____

_____

_____

_____

_____

_____

_____

_____

_____

_____

_____

My words come from an upright heart; my lips sincerely speak what I know.

Job 33:3

Reckless words pierce like a sword, but the tongue of the wise brings healing.

Proverbs 12:18

_____

_____

_____

_____

_____

_____

_____

_____

_____

_____

_____

_____

_____

_____

The tongue has the power of life and death, and those who love it will eat its fruit.

Proverbs 18:21

_____

_____

_____

_____

_____

_____

_____

_____

_____

_____

_____

_____

_____

*May the words of my mouth and the meditation of my heart
be pleasing in your sight, O Lord, my Rock, and my Redeemer.*

Psalm 19:14

_____

_____

_____

_____

_____

_____

_____

_____

_____

_____

_____

_____

A gossip betrays a confidence, but a trustworthy man keeps a secret.

Proverbs 11:13

_____

_____

_____

_____

_____

_____

_____

_____

_____

_____

_____

_____

_____

I have hidden your word in my heart that I might not sin against you.

Psalm 119:11

_____

_____

_____

_____

_____

_____

_____

_____

_____

_____

_____

_____

_____

Give thanks to the Lord, call on his name; make known among the nations what he has done.

1 Chronicles 16:8

_____

_____

_____

_____

_____

_____

_____

_____

_____

_____

_____

_____

_____

_____

_____

_____

Above all else, guard your heart, for it is the wellspring of life.

Proverbs 4:23

_____

_____

_____

_____

_____

_____

_____

_____

_____

_____

_____

_____

A word aptly spoken is like apples of gold in settings of silver.

Proverbs 25:11

_____

_____

_____

_____

_____

_____

_____

_____

_____

_____

_____

_____

_____

Your word is a lamp to my feet and a light for my path.

Psalm 119:105

_____

_____

_____

_____

_____

_____

_____

_____

_____

_____

_____

_____

_____

_____

_____

Pleasant words are a honeycomb, sweet to the soul and healing to the bones.

Proverbs 16:24

God is spirit, and his worshipers must worship in spirit and in truth.

John 4:24

_____

_____

_____

_____

_____

_____

_____

_____

_____

_____

_____

_____

_____

The king's heart is in the hand of the Lord; he directs it like a watercourse wherever he pleases.

Proverbs 21:1

_____

_____

_____

_____

_____

_____

_____

_____

_____

_____

_____

_____

_____

_____

By this all men will know that you are my disciples, if you love one another.

John 13:35

Do not let any unwholesome talk come out of your mouths, but only what is helpful for building others up according to their needs, that it may benefit those who listen.

Ephesians 4:29

But in your hearts set apart Christ as Lord. Always be prepared to give an answer to everyone who asks you to give the reason for the hope that you have.

1 Peter 3:15

_____

_____

_____

_____

_____

_____

_____

_____

_____

_____

_____

_____

You brood of vipers, how can you who are evil say anything good? For out of the overflow of the heart the mouth speaks.

Matthew 12:34

_____

_____

_____

_____

_____

_____

_____

_____

_____

_____

_____

_____

My words come from an upright heart; my lips sincerely speak what I know.

Job 33:3

———————————————————

———————————————————

———————————————————

———————————————————

———————————————————

———————————————————

———————————————————

———————————————————

———————————————————

———————————————————

———————————————————

———————————————————

———————————————————

Reckless words pierce like a sword, but the tongue of the wise brings healing.

Proverbs 12:18

_____

_____

_____

_____

_____

_____

_____

_____

_____

_____

_____

_____

_____

_____

The tongue has the power of life and death, and those who love it will eat its fruit.

Proverbs 18:21

_____

_____

_____

_____

_____

_____

_____

_____

_____

_____

_____

_____

_____

May the words of my mouth and the meditation of my heart
be pleasing in your sight, O Lord, my Rock, and my Redeemer.

Psalm 19:14

_____

_____

_____

_____

_____

_____

_____

_____

_____

_____

_____

_____

_____

A gossip betrays a confidence, but a trustworthy man keeps a secret.

Proverbs 11:13

I have hidden your word in my heart that I might not sin against you.

Psalm 119:11

Give thanks to the Lord, call on his name; make known among the nations what he has done.

1 Chronicles 16:8

_____

_____

_____

_____

_____

_____

_____

_____

_____

_____

_____

_____

_____

Above all else, guard your heart, for it is the wellspring of life.

Proverbs 4:23

_____

_____

_____

_____

_____

_____

_____

_____

_____

_____

_____

_____

_____

_____

_____

_____

A word aptly spoken is like apples of gold in settings of silver.

Proverbs 25:11

Your word is a lamp to my feet and a light for my path.

Psalm 119:105

_____

_____

_____

_____

_____

_____

_____

_____

_____

_____

_____

_____

_____

_____

Pleasant words are a honeycomb, sweet to the soul and healing to the bones.

Proverbs 16:24

God is spirit, and his worshipers must worship in spirit and in truth.

John 4:24

Talk It Up!

Want free books?
First looks at the best new fiction?
Awesome exclusive merchandise?

We want to hear from you!

Give us your opinions on titles, covers, and stories.
Join the Z Street Team.

Visit zstreetteam.zondervan.com/joinnow
to sign up today!

Also—Friend us on Facebook!

www.facebook.com/goodteenreads

• Video Trailers

• Connect with your favorite authors

• Sneak peeks at new releases

• Giveaways

• Fun discussions

• And much more!

ZONDERVAN®
.com